Acorn to Oak Tree

The Greatness You Seek is Inside You

Written by Benjamin Lawson

Acorn to Oak Tree
The Greatness You Seek is Inside you

ISBN: 978-1-7333709-0-5

Published by www.legacycoachingplus.com

Facebook: Legacy Coaching Plus

Instagram: Legacy Coaching Plus

Contents

Acknowledgements

I would like to thank some very special people that supported me throughout this journey of completing my first book. I would like to thank Jenny, my personal coach, who encouraged me and kept me accountable to a timeline to hit my completion goal for this book. I would like to thank my daughter, Maggie, who took the time to read my first draft and wrote an amazing forward for Acorn to Oak Tree. I left her writing in its original form to showcase how she spoke from her heart. It really touched me the first time I read it and it still warms my soul each time I read it. Also, I want to thank

Klemmer and Associates, a personal development and leadership development company, where I learned to embrace the greatness I carried inside me. I met so many fantastic people along my journey with this company who encouraged me, pushed me outside my comfort zone, and continue to support me as I keep working on my own legacy.

Finally, I want to thank Amanda. She provided such great feedback, insight, and tenderness around the direction of Acorn to Oak Tree. She also encouraged me to take this story outside the pages of this book and share it through speaking engagements so I could see first hand the kind of

legacy I am creating. Thank you to all of you for

your love and support.

<u>Forward by my daughter, Maggie, 11 years old</u>

(This is unedited and straight from her heart.)
Benjamin Lawson is a great leader, an excellent
mentor, and by far an outstanding dad. Through my
years of spending time with him, he's showed me
and taught me wonderful life lessons. Like this
book, "Acorn to Oak Tree," my dad showed me one
summer in Colorado how I can become a better
person, leader-wise and personality-wise.

Time to time, I became very angry with myself. I
said to me, "I can't do this! I'll never be able to,
either!!!" My dad saw I was frustrated with myself
for how I performed, so he taught me a great way to

handle my emotions such as anger or frustration. After that, I realized that even though I may get upset with myself, that doesn't make me a bad person. I was still special in his eyes, and I was still his little girl.

While my dad is a great mentor, he's also a wonderful father. We usually go on pretty big trips together, like when we went to the Bahamas. That trip is one I'll never forget! We had fun and got to spend lots of time together. I was really happy I was the one who got to do that with him, and I could really see how much he cared for me. He was the best dad in the world through my own two eyes.

While he loves spending time with his girl and helps calm down emotions, he's also a leader. No matter what problem he may be going through, my dad always seems to find a way out of it. He'll also help his fellow workers with a situation they may have or answer a question they've been puzzling about for a while. My dad knows how to get the right job done, and if you ask me, one of the best!!

My father is a stupendous man, no matter what point of view you look at him. He's kind and helpful, hardworking and honest, and loves to spend time with others. All dads are great, but Benjamin Lawson is one father, mentor, and leader that is one of the best.

Introduction

One bright sunny day I was visiting my parents at their country home in central Illinois and was suddenly struck by the awe and beauty of the oak tree in front of their home. It was tall and straight, the branches stretched out far from the trunk nearly parallel with the ground. It occurred to me that the tree was so much more than just a tree. It was a source of shade for the dog sleeping beneath it. It was a place to play for my nieces and nephew. The oak tree was also a home to different animals and insects.

Suddenly, while taking in this picture in time, a thought occurred to me. This mighty tree came from a nut that is about the size of the end of my thumb. The oak tree and all of its glory and gifts to this world came from a small plain acorn. Inside that little shell was all the greatness to create this tree, this provider to so many. And yet, when you look at the acorn, it is hard to see all of that.

Human beings, you and I, are the same as that oak tree. We come from a very small seed, and yet we have the opportunity to grow into so much more. We get to be overcomers, we can choose to be strong and resilient, we each are beautiful in our own special ways. All of this is inside of us and we get to decide how and when we tap into that greatness. The choice of how to use this greatness is what separates us from the mighty oak as it cannot choose to be something different. And yet, it is ready and fully prepared to act as soon as the opportunity presents itself to take hold and begin growing into that tree which provides so much to the space around it.

In this little book, much like the acorn, I want to share with you the "ah-ha" moment I had on that bright summer day gazing at the oak tree in front of my parent's house. I want to share about the greatness I found in me, the greatness that I thought had been lost after hitting a low point in my life. I discovered that greatness was waiting to be cultivated by me. It was waiting to be fed so it could take root once again and begin to grow, begin to spread. It was like the tiny acorn nut that gets dropped from the mighty oak and waits for the opportune time to sprout and begin its journey in this world. All the greatness of the tree housed inside and ready to take action.

And much like the life of the acorn to the oak, I have gone through trials and tribulations, both internal and external. I found an environment that provided fertile soil to grow my greatness with support and love, and just as the oak tree continues to grow year after year, I do so as well. My journey is far from over. And I believe that to really embrace the greatness in me, I get to be like that acorn: ready to take action when the opportunity presents itself, ready to overcome with strong resilience, and accept it's ok to be seen as a little nut when I'm going after a big dream!

It All Starts with a Tiny Seed

When you look at an oak tree, what do you see?
Most see the big tree standing tall and strong. The
branches stretched out providing shade for some
and a home to others. What most people do not
think about is where that tree came from. Have you
ever taken the time to stop and wonder how
something so large and wonderful came from such a
small seed about the same size as the end of your
thumb? All the greatness that we see in the tree was
housed in that tiny seed.

The acorn is the spark to greatness for the oak tree. It did not have to be motivated to become an oak tree. It did not wait for something else to come along and cheer it to victory. When the opportunity came to plant its roots and begin the journey from seed to a mighty oak, the acorn was prepared. Sure, there were things outside of the acorn that led to it having the chance to start the growth journey; and it was still fully prepared to begin when the opportunity came.

We are very much the same as that acorn. We are born with greatness inside us. It is there from the beginning. Everything we need to succeed in life comes into this world with us and we get to tap into that greatness when we want to. The distinct advantage we have from the acorn is we get to write our own story as to how we grow and who we become. We get to write our own story. One of the most important aspects of writing our story comes by being prepared for the opportunities that come our way.

The acorn is a little nut fully prepared for the opportunity to grow into the mighty oak. Are you prepared when opportunities knock? What are you doing right now that will set you up to run full speed ahead when the door is opened to a dream or goal you have been pursuing? An acorn, given the opportunity, grows roots first and establishes the anchor it will need to begin the growth stage of its life. It is usually 8-10 weeks before any growth is seen above the ground after an acorn is planted. When you look at your life, what roots are you planting? Are you reading personal growth books? Are you listening to success-centered podcasts? Are you spending time around people that build you up and encourage you to go after your dreams? Much like the acorn's physical roots provide important nutrients to the rest of the plant, the time you invest in yourself will feed your mind and heart the elements it desires to succeed. You get to choose to feed that greatness inside you to create a system of roots that will last a lifetime so you can stand firm when life throws obstacles your way.

When I found myself at a low point in my life, I was fortunate to have a friend and mentor that introduced me to a personal development company that taught me how to discover my greatness again. I attended my first seminar with them in 2015 and have continued to return on a regular basis. Every time I go back, I'm in a new place in my life so I get to discover something new about myself each time. It helped me get through that low point before I gave up on my dream and went back to being comfortable. I also started reading personal development books and listening to podcasts or YouTube videos from professional speakers that motivate and teach. I am constantly feeding my seed of greatness. You can choose to do the same thing. Keep feeding yourself the ingredients for greatness and the impact can be life-changing. I know it has been for me. Instead of throwing in the towel and going back to being comfortable, I chose to embrace the challenges as a way to grow, and when a new opportunity presented itself in my life, I was able to step into a position of leadership and impact all those around me.

Take that seed of greatness inside you and let it grow; nurture it, feed it, share it. Like the acorn be prepared for opportunities that are going to come your way. It is only a matter of time before one knocks on your door. It is your choice how you respond to the knock. Will you open the door and step out with courage knowing you have deep roots to keep you grounded? The little acorn only needs one shot to start its journey as it holds the greatness of the oak tree inside it. Embrace your oak tree and let your greatness grow.

Release your Greatness

1. If you knew you could not fail, what story would you write for your life?

2. How are you preparing yourself to be ready when an opportunity knocks?

3. What roots have you planted in your life?

4. If you don't like the roots you have planted, what can you do to change them?

The Greatness in the Seed

An acorn is stuffed with all the greatness it needs to begin its journey from a seed to an oak tree. Inside the shell, there are carbohydrates, proteins, and fats all ready to be used as the seed is planting its roots. At the beginning of this adventure, there are no leaves to support photosynthesis. It cannot rely on something else to feed it. The acorn is fighting for its spot in this world with all it has deep inside. Other than a little moisture through its roots, the acorn uses only the energy provided from its "guts." It uses up all it has until it can begin to feed itself from the environment around it.

Much like the acorn, we are filled with a greatness that can begin our journey of success. We are filled with dreams, goals, ambitions, and the courage to go after them. As a child, it seems we have no limits to our imagination. When was the last time you watched a child draw or play? Did you sit back and soak in their innocence and joy or did you find yourself thinking critical thoughts about how they were doing something incorrectly? That child was using their unbridled greatness to create an adventure of their own. How many times have you seen children take boxes or blankets and create castles or forts or some other place of magic and wonder? All of this is what we are born with. You had this greatness then, and you still do now.

When you begin to realize it is ok to be a little "nutty" now and then, amazing things can happen in your life. Begin to re-establish the roots you once had as a child. The amazing thing for you, compared to the acorn, you can start fresh any day. Today is a new day, and if you are not where you want to be in your life, you get to be like a brand new acorn fresh off the tree and dig deep into the greatness inside you to begin a new journey. Take a minute to do a gut check, harness all of that energy available to you when you want to use it, and set new roots for your adventure. An acorn has a 1 in 10,000 chance of growing into a mature oak tree. You have the power to decide if you are going to be successful. It is not by happenstance.

I used to worry about what I looked like in front of others. Not necessarily in a physical appearance, but what they would think about me if I acted a certain way. I feared being judged if I was too "silly" with my daughter in a public setting. In a professional setting, I was worried about how I would be judged when presenting to a crowd. We are usually our own worst critics, and this was especially true for me. I began attending Daddy-Daughter dances with my daughter from the time she was 5 years old. I was the typical dad. I stood around with the other dads until a slow song came on, then we would all go out and dance a song or two, and when it went back to faster songs, we would all make our way back to the sides while the girls ran around.

After I began to understand that this was a subconscious "program" running my actions, I was able to address it by looking at what the cost was by not taking full advantage of those one-night-a-year dances with my daughter. I realized I was missing precious opportunities to build life-long memories with Maggie. As I learned to embrace the fun and "nutty" times in my life, I now spend most of the dance in the center of the gym dancing in all kinds of silly ways with my daughter. The last dance we had together I had several other dads ask if I had taken dance lessons. I looked like I knew what I was doing! I've never had a lesson. I just chose to have fun and not worry about how I looked in anyone's eyes other than my daughter.

I do the same now for any occasion. When I am in front of a crowd, I stand there with confidence and share about the topic I am covering. I tap into that creativity that is there from my childhood. I use it to enjoy all those opportunities that come my way. If someone doesn't like my presentation, that is their choice. I truly believe I am impacting lives in a positive way by embracing my inner greatness.

You can begin tapping into this greatness in a handful of ways. Some of the most powerful ways to check in with yourself and ignite the greatness again are visual reminders, sharing it with people who support you and creating a system of accountability.

Have you ever created a dream board? A collage of pictures that include visual reminders you can look at every day will help you remember what is on the other end of your journey. There is no right or wrong way to make this. You can make digital dream boards or tap into your inner child and draw it out using crayons, markers, and colored pencils. You could make it into a family activity and have everyone make a dream board together. This can also be a way to ignite that greatness again by sharing it with people that love and support you. You get to share your dreams and goals with your spouse and children as you work on the dream boards together.

Find people around you that will encourage you to tap into your greatness. Share with them what you are feeling led to creating in your life. Again, there is no right or wrong way to do this. If your family supports you, tell them all about it. For those that grew up in a family where dreaming was frowned upon, find friends and mentors that will support you. The more people you tell about your dreams the larger the fire you are building to ignite your own greatness.

As you build that team of supporters, you can also create a way to hold yourself accountable. Those who truly care about you and want to see you succeed will encourage you and deliver some tough love when necessary. To really take hold of your greatness early in the journey means you will most likely be creating all-new habits. If your old habits were serving you in a successful way, you would likely have what you want in your life. Accountability partners and mentors will be able to remind you of your greatness while helping you see what is not serving you in your life.

You get to choose to be like that acorn. You get to be a little nutty as you dig deep into the greatness that you were born with while bringing people along on the journey that will support you being that nut!

Release Your Greatness

1. What visual reminders do you have around you to stimulate thoughts of greatness?

2. It has been said that we are the average of the 5 people we spend the most time with. Who are you spending time with? Are they encouraging you or stealing your dreams?

3. How do you respond when someone tries to hold you accountable to your commitments? Do you appreciate their feedback and support or do you become defensive?

Breaking Through Obstacles During Your Greatness Journey

When an acorn falls from the tree, the journey to becoming a mature oak tree has only just begun. It will encounter numerous obstacles in its first few days on the ground as it works to establish the roots. If the acorn is not harvested for winter food by a squirrel or eaten right away by a hungry wild pig, it will work to plant a tap root. This is the most important part of the root system as it goes down deep into the soil providing stability and nourishment when the sapling starts to sprout leaves and begins making food for itself.

Much like the acorn's tap root, what are you doing to anchor yourself in life? Who are you leaning on when obstacles show up? What do you do when you feel challenged? The taproot in your life is created at an early age. If it is tapped into negativity, hopelessness, and anger, it is probably safe to say your life doesn't look the way you want. If you are feeding yourself from areas like this, it is time to cut that taproot out of your life and create another. You have the choice to create a new taproot that will feed your mind, body, and soul what you want. The acorn uses its taproot to gather nutrients to help it grow. Create a tap root in your life that will serve you and your dreams using personal growth books and podcasts. Find a mentor who has what you want or who went through what you are going through and came out of the storm a stronger person. You are not stuck with the taproot that is in your life.

As the newly established oak sapling grows, it is constantly overcoming external factors. These external obstacles are out of its control while it is growing to become the mighty oak tree it is destined to be. The weather could be too dry or too wet. Animals such as deer enjoy the sweet young leaves of young tree saplings. The soil could be too hard. Even competition from other plants and trees could affect the outcome of the tiny oak tree. With all of these factors working against the sapling, it is easy to see now only 1 in 10,000 acorns make it from the seed to the mature oak.

What you can learn from this little seed is the key to success. The secret is the focused energy the sapling has while establishing itself in the forest. Early in its life, all the energy is used to break through its first barrier, the ground, and create the taproot. As it sprouts into a sapling and begins to feed itself, the tiny oak tree will lean towards the light. It soaks up as much as it can to produce food through photosynthesis. It keeps growing towards the light, consistently doing the same thing each day. The tree is naturally built to do what it takes to be successful during its life cycle. It does not matter what obstacles come at it, the consistency of the sapling's growth will lead to a mature tree. Some years might be a little slower growth and other years will set records on how much growth was achieved. It is the growth, no matter how big or small, that leads to the end result it wants.

This acorn to sapling journey is parallel to what your new adventures will be like. You can expect to have life throw obstacles at you when you begin. There will be outside influences that will try to derail what you want to accomplish. This is where you get to harness the greatness inside of you and focus on what you can control: yourself. You get to control how you react to life's obstacles. There is an old saying that life is 10% what happens to you and 90% how you react to it. How do you react when an obstacle comes at you? If your reaction is not what you want in your life then perhaps it is time to look at where your taproot is anchored.

I found myself focused on everything that was going wrong about halfway through 2014. I was still a new financial advisor working on a commission scale and found myself with very little cash flow. Looking back I was not doing what was necessary to be successful in that type of career when I was in that position. My response to all of that was to complain about the system being broke and not fair instead of looking in and asking myself what I could do to change the situation. I was choosing a victim a card rather than taking responsibility. My taproot was anchored in negativity at that point in my life and a feeling of hopelessness. I chose to move out of my apartment after missing a few months of rent and into a make-shift apartment my parents put together for me in the workshop my dad was using for his construction business.

As the holidays neared, I did not have the money to buy gifts for my daughter and had to borrow $150 from my brother to get a few things for her. In my mind, I was failing as a dad. I could not provide for the one person who was most important in my life. At least, that is how I looked at it during the time. It was a dark time for me when I was normally a positive person who looked for the silver lining in most situations. Fortunately, I had a manager that cared for the people on his team just as much, if not more, than the business that was being written. When I was ready to throw in the towel on a career that looked very promising for me in the beginning, he provided guidance and support to get me through the tough times. I started to see a turn around in my business and soon after I was invited to a personal development seminar I referenced earlier in the book.

I began to change my focus after that seminar on what I wanted out of life instead of where I was currently. I looked for the light. I reached out for support. I stayed plugged in with more seminars and began reading books to further my personal development. I spent my energy on growing myself first, and soon after my business as a financial advisor began to exponentially grow eventually leading to an opportunity to be a leader in the firm as a training manager. I used my story to provide support and motivation for new advisors as they learned how to build their own business as well.

Where are you spending your energy? The acorn to the sapling tree spends energy on its growth, on its development into a larger and stronger tree. Are you spending your energy on a negative attitude? Are you focused on all the obstacles that are coming at you? If that is where your focus is the majority of what you see will be the obstacles. That is where I was in my life. Change your focus to the possibilities around you and look for the light in your life. Identify what the light is in your life that drives you: spiritual, family, friends, etc. Begin your day with gratitude for what you have and what you are going to have as you continue to grow in your greatness.

Obstacles will never stop even as you mature in your journey. That is why it is so important to find a mentor or coach that can support you in discovering all the greatness you possess. It is your choice as to how much you want to tap from inside. Focus on yourself and what you can control, your learning and personal development, and you will find that the greatness goes so much deeper than you could ever imagine.

Release Your Greatness

1. What emotions and energy is your tap root pulling into your life?

2. What is your usual reaction when an obstacle pops up on your road to success?

3. Where is your focus each day? Are you thinking about what you don't want to happen or is your focus on what you want each day?

Big Growth as a Sapling

During the young years of an oak tree's life cycle, there is a lot of big growth happening. The tree is constantly adding more limbs, expanding the reach of its branches, getting a larger base in its trunk, and as all of this is happening the taproot is getting deeper and the root system as a whole is expanding. This is constant and consistent growth. We do not see a young tree grow quickly in one direction and stop. Sprout new limbs and suddenly go in a different direction. You will not see the "stop and go" effect with these majestic trees.

During these years of tremendous growth, the tree also maintains a level of flexibility. As the winds blow and the other trees around change the angle at which light filters through the forest, the young oak tree stays consistent and flexible to get into the best possible position for more growth. You do not see a young tree suddenly drop its leaves and stop growing when something in its environment changes (barring something extreme like total devastation of the land it is in). The tree remains constant, makes adjustments, and keeps growing, working toward the end result of a mature oak tree. At this time of growth and flexibility, there are times when the young oak tree doesn't look much like the mighty oaks around it. It might not have the branch spread and it still isn't producing any acorns of its own. It is still an oak tree at the core and it will look however it is supposed to on the day it matures. When that day happens, it will be a magnificent tree of its own accord.

When you go after your own dreams and goals there will be times when things don't look like how you imagined. Perhaps you thought a new business venture was going to involve your two best friends and you would be life long partners together, building your fortune. When you approached them, they were not interested and wish you the best of luck. Does that mean your dream of being a

business owner is not going to happen? No, it

means you get to step into other possibilities and

create partnerships from somewhere else. Or maybe

you get to create a new business all on your own.

The important piece of this example is that you

believe in yourself and the greatness you already

possess.

Much like the young oak tree, you can choose to be

flexible during these times. The ability to be

flexible, to flow with the process of growth and

discovery, allows you to keep growing without

breaking. You get to discover how much greatness

you have while you grow and develop during these times. The key is to keep growing. Constant steady growth will support you as you seek out new opportunities.

If you start a new project and choose to pursue it in a sporadic style, it will be much harder to commit to the project. It takes a lot of energy to start over every time. Consistent activity is the key to successful growth. When life throws you a curveball, much like can happen to young oak trees, the growth might slow at times yet it still does not stop. You feed yourself even more during those times through an established routine of personal development. Creating this routine when times are good will make it easier to maintain when the obstacles increase.

To support your growth create a vision of where you are going. Think about what your purpose is in life. When we look at the acorn to the sapling to the young oak tree, it's clear what the purpose is: become a mature oak tree. You get the opportunity to discover your purpose in life as you grow and harness your greatness. There is no right or wrong purpose; it is your own. Even though the details of how it looks might change throughout your journey of discovery, at its core, you will see a theme that has been there your entire life. Harnessing the greatness inside you will allow that purpose to shine even brighter while you pursue your vision.

Keep your vision fresh in your mind and in your heart. Know where you are going and what you want to achieve. When you embrace your greatness your vision begins to align with your purpose. When this happens you can create amazing results. The obstacles in life no longer knock you off your path like they used to. The growth that occurs during this time leads to large changes in your life bringing you closer to your vision becoming a reality. You get to stay laser-focused and pour your energy into creating what you want.

As you achieve the results you want, you get the opportunity to set more goals and keep moving forward so your growth does not stagnate. As a former national champion football coach, author and speaker Lou Holtz said, "In this world, you're either growing or you're dying so get in motion and grow." Keep growing and keep feeding yourself. Personal growth will provide tools for you to break through the obstacles in life and prepare you for the opportunities that are coming your way. Speaker and author Les Brown has said, "It is better to be prepared for an opportunity and not have one than to have an opportunity and not be prepared." Keep a learner's mind for yourself and approach everything with the idea that you can learn something new no matter your background.

In my own life, I have written several visions that span from 1 year to 20 years. It tends to work best when sitting in a quiet place, especially if you can get out in nature and really open your mind to possibility. I found a theme that shows up in nearly every writing even though it might look a little different each time. I don't question what shows up on the paper. I read it, reflect on it, and get excited about what the future might hold. I look at it with that child-like excitement I referred to in my previous chapters. I am committed to my personal growth journey because I know that as I grow and keep tapping into my own greatness, the opportunity to see these potential outcomes in my life increase dramatically. I believe there is power in writing out these visions and encourage everyone to find the time to do it. Let your imagination take over and you might be surprised what shows up on your paper!

Release Your Greatness

1. Where in your life would additional flexibility support you?

2. Do you finish what you start? How many times do you start, stop, and start again on a single project?

3. Write a 1, 3, and 5-year vision for your life. Include all the success your going to accomplish during that time. Don't be shy and don't hold back. Dream big here and have fun!!

The Mature Oak Tree

Many species of oak trees take as long as 20 to 30 years to fully mature and begin producing acorns. Some might see this statistic and feel what a long time to wait before getting anything back from the tree. The acorns provide food for animals and are the seed to provide for new trees. This is all true, and the years leading up to the fruit-producing time has not been lost. The tree was still providing to the area around it in other ways. Animals and insects can use the tree for shelter. On a hot day, it provides shade for those around it. The non-acorn bearing oak tree can even provide hours of entertainment for children and adults alike as they climb and swing on the branches.

As the tree matures to the age in which it can produce acorns, it can now be viewed as something that creates more like itself. It is the same for you as you are growing and developing over the years. When you are young in your personal development story, it might not seem like you are producing much fruit other than for yourself. You are working to grow yourself, you rely on mentors and coaches to support you as you get to the next level of development.

As you choose to step into personal growth you are creating an example for others to follow. You are blazing a path for those around you to follow that can also change their lives in outstanding ways. They are using your "branches" to climb up. They are creating excitement in their lives just as the children do on the oak tree. Your new outlook on life spills over at work and in your home that leads to better relationships in both places. Your focus might still be on you and your own growth, and you are still impacting people in your circle of influence. It is similar to how the oak tree impacts the area around it without actually producing seeds yet. You are more mature and have the grounding necessary to be the strong, humble leader no matter the venue.

And just like the oak tree that will bear acorns to continue its legacy, you too will be able to complete the circle that began with you discovering the greatness inside you. You will have the opportunity to support others as they begin to discover their greatness creating a legacy of life-changing opportunities that will stretch beyond your lifetime if you so choose.

I have had the opportunity to impact lives in so many ways. On a daily basis, I get to impact my daughter, Maggie, in a way that I cannot measure. I would be a great dad to her no matter what my situation, and I know I am an even better and stronger dad to her because I chose to begin a journey into rediscovering my own greatness. I have a relationship with her now such that she knows she can come to me with anything and I will be there for her. She used to be afraid to tell me small things thinking I would get upset over it. Now, she comes to me with any question or concern, and on any topic, believing that I am going to work through it with her. I can talk freely with her about how I feel with my love, joy, and excitement during our adventures. I can also express when I am disappointed or upset with her in a way that she knows I am doing so as a loving father.

I have coached countless peers at work on both business-related topics and personal topics when they are struggling with areas outside of the office. They understand they are not just a number at a company. I have been able to connect with them and lead them to the level of success they want with their financial advising practice. I have also stepped into coaching individuals on a one-to-one basis after earning a life coaching certification. I have also had the opportunity to share my story through a handful of speaking engagements to provide hope and motivation to those in attendance. When I was feeling broken down and saw no light at the end of the tunnel in 2014, I never imagined I would be in the position I am in today. I get to tap into the greatness I was born with on a daily basis as I work on leaving a legacy of impacting lives and creating opportunities for growth. This is the fruit I am producing now. These are the acorns I am dropping around me with the hope that they can establish their taproots and harness their own greatness.

When you are ready to tap into your greatness, you can find additional resources on my website at www.legacycoachingplus.com and also on my social media platforms. I am on Facebook, Instagram, and I have a YouTube channel with inspirational messages and personal development pieces to support you as you continue on your journey. All social media platforms are also under Legacy Coaching Plus. You can reach out to me through my website to learn more about my coaching programs and speaking engagements. I want to hear about the success you are creating in your life as you tap more and more into your greatness! Here's to living as a little "nut"!

Release Your Greatness

1. Where have you missed opportunities because of your limited focus?

2. Everyone is a leader in some capacity. Who are you blazing a path for and how?

3. What is the first step you can take today that will begin your journey to reigniting your greatness?